DEDICATION

In memory of my grandmother Leah Nora Carter
Williams, MeMe Marshall, my great grandmother,
Albert Spencer Suddlow, my principal in elementary
school, who told me there was no such word as 'I can't'.
He said, "You can do anything you want."

Also, to Dr. Alan Kay, New York City Community College,
who told me, "Write what you want to write, write
what you feel, a writer must write what he has to
write."

THE UNLIMITED MIND

by *Hyacinth Williams-Moncrieffe*

with a foreword by Melvin Cunningham

Cyber Clerical Associates, LLC

Cover designed by Bill Waithe.
Other illustrations by Bill Waithe.
Back cover photo by Kingsley Grant.
Typesetting & mechanicals by Louis Reyes Rivera.
Editorial Consultant: Louis Reyes Rivera
Set in Theme 10/11.
Printed in the United States of North America.

Telling Too Much, first published in 1978 by WBAI Folio. *Rats And Roaches In Bedford Stuy*, and *Addiction*, first published 1979 by WABI Folio. *Refuse To Accept Your Culture's Pride*, first published in 1980 by Universal Black Writer Magazine. *Black Cries* first published in 1981 by The Universal Black Writer Magazine.
Two Steps Over Please, *The Protection*, *Realistically Delving*, first appeared in the anthology *Black And In Brooklyn*, 1983, The Universal Black Writer Press.

Publisher: *Cyber Clerical Associates, LLC, Kissimmee, FL*

FOREWORD

Here you have another writer fashioning her truth. Happily, Hyacinth Williams-Moncrieffe does so in this volume with a sense of public mission. You would be right in saying that she was fired up by the same human emotion called *discontent* and *yearning* that burn in other people. It would be inaccurate, however, to say that her metrics and rhythms are facsimiles of comparable writers. Hers has a personal style.

As she unlocks her heart you see her facing various life situations- reluctant to ask only "Why?" You can hear her snapping this question instead, "Why not?" Her words echo possibilities. Meanwhile, she works with familiar topics like mother, eyes, bus, and shoes, but blends them fittingly with eternal verities. She caresses Justice and gives birth to Compassion.

So, you are given this opportunity to relish the work of Hyacinth Williams-Moncrieffe in the theater of these pages. And your presence spells encouragement for another writer to let her truth go searching, as it springs with candor and zest.

Melvin Cunningham
May, 1983

TABLE OF CONTENTS

ACKNOWLEDGEMENTS

[This book could or may not have been possible without several motivating people]

Miss Linda Cousins who encouraged me, made it possible for my voice to heard sometimes after I'd given up. For introducing me to the Black United Front. Thanks to Rev. Daughtry and Brother Bernard Sneid for making it possible for me to perform and deliver the message that I am sent to deliver.

Miss Edna Seivwright and all the other radio interviewers who had me on their shows: Miss Carla Burns, Medgar Evers College Radio; Miss Marie Haylock, National Black Network; Mr. Gill Bailey, WHBI, WBAI. And others.

To several professors of St. Joseph's College in Brooklyn, NY who gave me the opportunity to perform before their classes. Also, to the many students who were my classmates.

To my family, my mother, who taught me to read and write at an early age. To my children who tolerated me emotionally, particularly when the going was rough in compiling this volume – my girls Denise & Max (ine), that pitched in with, typing, drawing, and binding the books to their covers...using glue. A full, family effort.

To all my friends, the staff on the job. To Miss Castellie who gave me the privilege to recite my poem in the nursing office although they were busy. Special thanks to a friend, a co-worker who pressured me to publish this book before I was ready to. "Borrow the money," said Mrs. Hyacinth Illidge, "even a loan but do it. People must hear your work."

1.

Courage

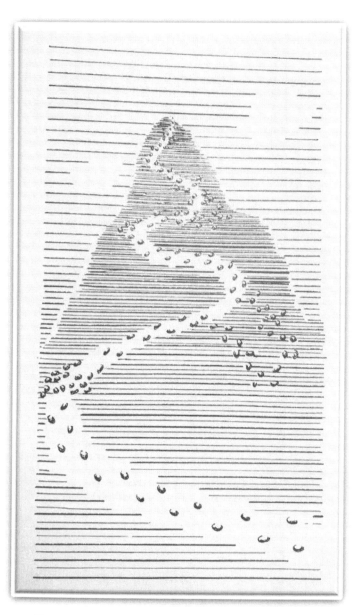

Illustration by: Hyacinth William-Moncrieffe

THE UNLIMITED MIND

Man shall never stop to seek
Knowledgeable zeals of great intrigues
The highest of heights ever to climb vastly
Seeks to be ahead of his time.

A clock how constantly it ticks
Solving problems of intensive wit
Delaying actions, creating plans, borrowing
Time from everyone. Time is the greatest master
Ruler, dictator of man. Man, always seeks to be
Ahead of his time.

Energy escapes before and after birth
Takes its rightful place with ulterior
Alert. This little unintelligible human being
Dominating utero before it's seen. Energy, Energy,
Energy saliently flows-Analyzing! the mind with
intensive glow. Man shall never stop to seek
Knowledgeable zeals of great intrigues.

THE ARRIVAL OF A HUMAN BEING

The arrival of a minute human being
How beautiful that moment should have been
To some that moment was never seen. The arrival
of a pretty, bloody, tender, human being.

The arrival of a lovely human being
Brought -- in a world packed with negative and
Traumatic scenes. The arrival of a minute, pretty,
tender, bloody, human being.

The arrival of an unwanted child
Brought - in a world to fulfill some selfish drams
Disrespected, unloved, by other human beings,
searching!
seeking! a place to rescue in the arrival of a tender,
Pretty, bloody, minute, human being.

The arrival! of a definite human being
A dual combination early may not seen.
Came - to a world with a mind that is clean.
Environ-
mental duration polluted his dreams. The arrival
of a
Tender, pretty, bloody, minute, human being.

RATS AND ROACHES IN BED-STUY

I think I hear them coming,
their footsteps how I dread.
Too many marks they left behind,
I scald them till they're dead.

I look down when I see them, and
even when I don't. For I think they
will be coming, even when they won't.

Too bad they aren't going to surprise
me, not any more they don't.
For I set some food up for them, to entice them
where and when.

Alas! I caught a number of them, as they
crawled under the couch. And then I saw Denise
hit
them, and their bellies like a pouch. *"Squeek-
Squeek!"*,
I heard them crying, and the sound of the music
blend.

*'I AM WEARING A DIFFERENT PAIR OF SHOES

The world had done me great injustice
I have paid my dues
The more I try the harder it is to prove
I gave my best, it was not good enough
You requested and requested and requested
I have paid my dues, myself I no longer
have to prove. I will never again be used.
I am wearing a different pair of shoes.

I forever always stand justly with the
Constitution in my hand. It says I'm an equal man.
I am a citizen of this land. No longer
will I sit in the rear of the bus,
give up my seat because others say I must. I have
paid my dues. Myself I no longer have to prove. I
will never again be used. I am wearing a different
pair of shoes.

I am a shiny black stallion.
Your perfect model of a sparkling diamond.
Obsessed with the color of my skin, the limit –

Less merits that creativity brings. I have paid my dues. Myself I no longer have to prove. I will never again, be used. I am wearing a different pair of shoes.

I give, you want

I give, you want

You want, you want, you want

The parasites that extract my blood

Deplete the iron content from my bones, to severe

state of anemia

I have paid my dues; myself I no longer have to prove. I

will never again be used. I am wearing a different pair of shoes.

I cannot walk

I cannot talk

I cannot run

I cannot hear

I cannot see

Unable to recognize my family.

The world had done me a great injustice

I have paid my dues. Myself I no longer

have to prove. I am a citizen of this land
Fighting justly with the constitution in
my hand. It says I'm an equal man
Never, never, never again will I be used
I am wearing a different pair of shoes.

'Dedicated to Doris Turner, President of District 1199
(1983)

BLACK CRIES

Black cries - -! flowing, raining in Atlanta.

It's sated in The Universal Black Writer.

Genocide --! Genocide. Black children eliminated

By sociopathic snipers.

What can the poor people do?

They are crying for a better living condition too.

"There is going to be hell in these Ghettos." Ben

Vereen–dramatic at presidential inauguration;

impresses minds with tension.

Retrospectively. Presently. Futuristically.

Seeing. Hearing Black cries–Black cries

in America.

Black cries

all over the world.

Black cries! - - flowing, raining in Harlem.

Rev. Jesse Jackson gives them a warning.

NAACP is alarming.

What can the poor people do?

They are crying for a better living condition too.

"There is going to be hell in these Ghettos."

Their children running around with hungry
bellies.

Too much poverty marks the inner cities. "There is

going to be hell in these Ghettos."

Retrospectively. Seeing. Hearing.

Black cries - -! Black cries

in America.

Black cries

all over the world.

Black cries - -! flowing, raining in Florida.

Standing, watching my brothers' murder, Justice -
-!

Your body, my body, shaped, touched, molded

by the same Creator.

Retrospectively, presently, futuristically,

Seeing, hearing, Black Cries - -! Black cries

in America.

Black cries

all over the world.

'REGULAR MERITS

Give me what I deserve, since I've worked hard for
it

I have toiled hard all day long, til' sweat ran

Down my brow, and salty taste lined my mouth,
yet

you have given, regular merits.

Toiling hard without sleep, eight straight nights

and days. Now my body is broken down and

ooooooooooh, my poor aching feet. Give me what I

deserve please, don't give me regular merits.

You had what you wanted to put me down, but I
know

what I can do. Now I have seen sparkling crowns
and

you confirmed it too. Still, you want to put me
down.

You have given, regular merits.

Could it be the color of my skin? I can't help it!

God knows it's true. Give me what I deserve
please,

don't give me regular merits.

I know I am going to have trouble with you,

I am black and thirty-two. You are a white
professor and sixty-two.

And all-l-l-l-l-l-l my chances are dead with you.

Is that all you know how to do? Giving people

regular merits.

*Dedicated to Ms. Bishop, a teacher (6th Grade - at my
daughter Max's elementary school) at Elijah J. Stroud,
Public School 316, Brooklyn, NY.*

DR. ALAN KAY

I think of you like a capitalist
Who don't care who earns his money?
A long as he gets his share. This
I know belongs to you, you are doctor,
Doctor Alan Kay.

You are a teacher! A teacher indeed.
Not many like you, you'll find around.
You gave each one his assignment and
Graded them fair. This I know belongs
To you, you are doctor, Doctor Alan Kay.

You didn't ask where we are from, color
Of skin, or where we belong. You gave us
All your knowledge, knowing that at
Sixty-five, you'll be out and I maybe in.
This I know belongs to you, you are doctor,
Doctor Alan Kay.

Three years have passed since I've been around.
Never one like you could be found. Summer is
here, we will be apart,
You will be missed! You will be missed,
Dear doctor, Doctor Alan Kay.

BRAIN-DRAIN

Brain-drain
Brain-drain
At the ending of semester
You are a busy, busy bee
Surrendering term papers to each and every
single professor
Brain-drain
Brain-drain
At the ending of semester

Do not ask what I have learned
Most times recollection of only few words
Objectives tests left no traces on my mind
Memories of subjective tests daily helps
Along the line
Brain-drain
Brain-drain
At the ending of semester

No texts or books do I want to see
In my sleep they crowded powerlessly
Give me fun
Give me leisure
Let me have some social pleasure
Keep your books, reports, researches till
The middle of next semester
Brain-drain
Brain-drain
At the ending of semester

Don't dare ask what's the matter
Let's have fun and social pleasure
A plain ticket I'd rather have
Scurry on a big jet to sunny Jamaica

Cocooned to the touches, grace of
Caribbean fever.
Brain-drain
Brain-drain
At the ending of semester

Taking sun-baths on white, silvery sand
Drenching mind romantically with music
Of various Reggae bands
The tugging drumming give birth to island
Watch flying fishes spinning, jumping, dancing
On fishermen's reels
Bless your soul with fiery Calypso, Folk Limbo,
Rumba dancers
Drinking rum and coconut at my leisure
Brain-drain
Brain-drain
At the ending of semester

There are many, many exotic beautiful places
things for us to see
This beautiful world created by Nature for
You and me
If you have time, check the Blue Lagoon
You are bound to fall in love very soon
A guided tour under Fern Gully disentangles
my mind, later helped me to study
Brain-drain
Brain-drain
At the ending of semester

Just stroll with me along Puerto Seco
See the décor of Columbus Harbor
The glass-bottom boats savor reflections
In sky-blue, transparent water; affects the mind

calmly with peaceful slumber
Brain-drain
Brain-drain
At the ending of semester

POLLUTION

Big and small smoke seeps daily from your
walls.

The ocean beneath its bodies, engulfs it all
Daily accumulations pile just as tall.

Degenerating animals, birds, and all. You will
outlive me.

I am not a wall.

CLANISH DYNASTY

Having not a place to go

Someone in this audience stole my show.

Yet none blink an eye, say a word, or turn a head.

The coalition for century reigns.

A clannish dynasty maintains.

But if I live for a thousand years,

I will damn them to eternity. No one,

No one blink an eye; say a word, turn a head,

Yet they stripped me of my pride,

My dignity, my royalty, to maintain their
monarchy.

A clannish dynasty maintained.

I'M NOT READY YET

A fight. A fight kept to the end

Looked in the eyes of evening tide

Dusk peeked- -said I'm not ready yet,

I'm not ready yet

There is so much work to be done, and

Sir! You are calling me from my fun

I am not ready yet, I am not ready yet

It's my only wish to conquer you

Those horrible mistaken experiences you put me
through

Just one more chance to complete my task

I'll answer you only, then at last

I am not ready yet, I am not ready yet

But you and I know full well that you can

never be misled. Your games we play, your

wages you pay. Diplomacy used to limit your days

There are so much tasks to be done

You are extrapolating my fun

I am not ready yet, I am not ready yet

POOR MAMA

The clock alarms at seven

Mother no longer in heaven

Waking all the children

Tucking ribbons in their hair

Hustling and bustling, getting

Things done. Father in in the

kitchen eating, reading, and having fun

Mother dear, mother dear, that's not

fair.

I AM YOU

I am you, unable to be me
Since you insist that I be you instead
of being me
I wonder how it feels to have one's own identity.

Autonomy, liberty should set me free
Yearning to be me holistically
Credits ascertain only given in my name
They are always given to have one's own identity

Conflicts occur fulfilling your goals and mine
But often they run parallel from time to time
Deviating to explore life my biological rights are
mine. Robbed of many experiences, infancy,
toddler, Teenage, middle life, and even
senescence
I wonder how it feels just to be me
I know how it feels to identify with you
When I see myself, I will think it's you.
I wonder how it feels to have my own identity

THE ABUSED CHILD

I see a little black girl without shoes on her feet

I see a little black boy with not enough to eat

There is no job for mother to exchange her labor

No job for father where he can earn a dollar

Mama and Papa sat weeping, crying mad as hell

I see mother's pair of shoes landing on the boy's
head

Another poor black child is abused, will he be the

category of the "Abused Who Are Dead?"

Another statistic - -

Numbers, computerized numbers.

ONLY WANT A JOB TO BUY SOMETHING TO EAT

A man thinks he's high, builds his house
in the sky, refuses to look at a beggar, at his feet.
Ha! Ha! ah! ah! ah! laughs the beggar,
I'm only asking for a job, to buy something to eat.

Life is not only for the rich, it's also for
the poor. Life is not only for the high,
there is the median and the low. Life's not only
for the tall, but the ruler of us all
I only want a job, to buy something to eat.

You commute by express train; I commute via
local
You may wear a three-piece business suit; I'm
wearing an ordinary plaid.
Your life and my life, seem to be going in many
directions.
We both have a one-way ticket, to the same
destination.
All I want is a job, to buy something to eat.

I was a bright young man when I entered your
office door
You said I had no experience or contributions to
make
And all the other doors, slammed in my face
It seems they formed a coalition. They all said
the same, "Don't call me, I will call you."
All I want is a job to keep my family off the street.

I don't need charity or government playing big
Bother me. I don't need government playing
Papa to my children. I need to maintain my
manhood to support my family. I'm in great

competition with the welfare in this country.
It supports my children, and is Papa to them.
You refuse to give me a job; label me nigger, lazy
bummer on the street. All I want is a job to support
my family. All I want is a job, so that my woman
and my children can respect me.
All I want is a job, to buy something to eat.

Life my friends is very magical. I do not have
finances to consult a psychiatrist. I do have the
money to pay my medical bills. I have no other
means or places to get therapy. My situation then
forces me to resort to magic therapy.
All I want is a job, to buy something to eat.

We will meet again, on a broader yet a narrower
street.
On that street, there will be no prejudice. On that
street,
no one cares about your big business suit. On that
street,
we are the little stones, rocking, bouncing against
each other
There'll be no labels for me, for you to be placed.
There'll be no feelings or humility. No first-class,
middle-class, second-class citizens.
All I want is a job, to feed my family.
All I want is a job, so they can respect me. All I
want is a job, to buy something to eat.

TELLING TOO MUCH

I know you are lonely, yes, I said
But woman, woman watch your friends
Chatting-Chatting, all the time try
and find another source. Three nights
in a row, she dreamt of him, then she
said, it's a coincidence. Last thing before
you retired to bed, coy long-lost thoughts
were suppressed.

FEAR OF DEATH

Dying, lying, at death's door

The lady groans, her voice, it soars

"What's the matter?" asked the nurse

"What do you want", the reply came fast

There was a pause ---

I got to settle my problem with my bro–

They're one-hundred, one hundred, one hundred
dollars

The nurse left the room, the call-bell rang soon.

She went in, answered again.

"What can I do for you madam?" "Just turn;

me a little; I'm lying on my hand."

The nurse looked with angry eyes

Turned the lady with quick disguise.

"Is there anything else I can do for you?

Will you tell me before I'm through?"

Nothing, nothing as meek as a child she said.

"Then have a pleasant goodnight," quoted the
nurse as she read.

The bell rang before she reached the foot of
The bed. "What can I do for you?' the nurse angrily
yelled. This damn lady gets to my head. "You
rang, you rang the doggone bell?" The dying old
lady closed her eyes, uttered the words, "I'm not
well." Before the nurse turned her back, her eyes
closed. The nurse cried, she cried, she yelled,
"Just a minute! Just a minute with her I want to
spend." The doctors came, pronounced her dead.

CRAZY JERK

A man in bells came down the aisle
He said, "I know you want me gal."
"Are you the beautiful girl in twelve,
That I heard them talking about?"

I didn't realize I was answering him
Until I saw my feet. I swing to the left,
I swing to the right.

Oh,
Yay! It got to be the boogie-man!
Yay! It got to be the boogie-man!

MOVING UP IN THIS WORLD

Days waited patiently for friends to return your
calls
No one knocks any longer on your front door,
no one thinks of you at all. Not even the man from
your friendly store. You are moving up in this
world. Moving up in this world.

Selected many activities to occupy your mind, one
that is unsatisfied.
Mails were placed in your neighbor's box. But
yours? An empty piece of metal slot. Each day the
children check. They check the box, to them it
was quite a shock.
You are moving up in this world, moving up in this
world.

A child, she came rushing in, got from the slot,
what was within.
An advertisement it was–for slip-covers.
These are the words, my daughter said,
"Mommy, don't your fiends write or call you
anymore?'
"Mommy, this is the last day this will occur. You
will get a letter every day, even when the mail is
on holiday."
You are moving up in this world, moving up in this
world.

I did not believe the child.
I could not believe the child.
For some reason, I don't know why.
To my surprise, it was the last day, that a letter did
not arrive.

For the rest of the year, a letter came. Each and
every one, bore my name.
The bold prints clearly seen on them:
"Happy Mother's Day, Happy Post Mother's Day,
Happy Easter, Christmas, New Year,
Happy Summer Day, Happy Spring Day, Happy
Birthday.
You are moving up in this world, moving up in this
world.

Each illustrates a great part of my life. The prints
of bright crayons,
Pen, pencil, marker, they look right. I read,
"Mommy, Mommy, you are a Good Mommy. You
wash my clothes, cook my food, love me and tuck
me to bed. Mommy I really love you. I want no one
to hurt you again.
You are moving up in this world, moving up in this
world.

The cards, the letters came every day in the metal
box, without a stamp they lay. Mommy, Mommy,
the last one I received said,
"Mommy, I'll be your lover, your friend, your
daughter. I will call every day, even when the
mailman is on holiday."
"Mommy I really love you. I want no one to hurt
you again."
You are moving up in this world, moving up in this
world.

Dedicated to my youngest child, Max.

THE AGED TREE

The tree is young,

It blooms wild flourishes,

Life decks with age no longer sprouts

The leaves don't send,

The bows they bend,

Even when nourishes it no longer flourishes.

It's withered, it's dry,

The bark on the trunk don't stick,

Elasticity just lies.

Oh! Dear tree, came the forest cry.

We love thee, we love thee

The voices came closer as they cried.

I cannot tarry, the old tree moaned

My time is come, please let me be gone.

Why waste your breath,

Precious nutrients on me?

Give it, give it, to some other tree.

The soil it cracks all around my husk

No strength support, no guardian musk.

The wind it blows

Seeps through my bows.

They shiver and shake, how transparently they
ache.

So why! waste your precious nutrients on me?

So, what's a tree?

Sometimes how important it might be,

When it's dead, please let it be.

There is no use from a dead old tree.

IS THIS THE WAY, HOW COMMUNITY PRAISE?

Our abodes are in the same vicinity.

Our domains a web entangled by social

Activities.

Could this be classified as a community?

Perplexities, anxieties, of human fears, shared in
the same flats, very near.

Whether we like it or not, this is one of the places,
where we call the shots.

Is this one of the ways, how our community praise?

Africans, West Indians, Jews, Europeans, it doesn't

matter where you are from, we all migrated to the
same land.

You don't want to come to my town, I don't want
to go to your town,

Because skin is either black, white, or brown.

Couldn't life be more easy to understand? Is this

one of the reasons, why we cannot live as one?

Eliminate the world of conflicts, it seems that man
would have no fun.

Shuffling-Shuffling in this land, United States of
America.

Keeping distance from one another. Is this one of
the ways how community praise?

Our standards, they lie, society makes them high.

The goals of competition sometimes make you cry.

You may never reach that height. You are
defeated, keep on trying.

Not because they did not sympathize with you,

Is this why you try to eliminate your society,
setting fire to your neighbor's house?

No place to sit, no one with whom to talk.

No accommodation, for you at all. Is this one of the
ways how community praise?

HOW CAN YOU DEPRIVE ME OF A HAPPY HEART?

It is imminent that I will depart

How can you deprive me of a happy heart?

A last sip, a last puff with or without it, I will
depart

ha! ha! ha! ha! you are my decision-maker,

my selector, lead the way grand-master.

Just two more decades, your will be made, by

someone sitting in your chair, by the rules

concocted, by you and your peers

How can you deprive me of a happy heart?

It is imminent that I will depart. A last sip,

a last puff. What's the matter with that?

ha! ha! ha! ha! you are my decision-maker,

my selector, lead the way grand-master.

HUNGER IN MY SOUL

O' burning hunger in my soul, I'm trying to escape from thee.

How far can I run the thoughts on my mind they be.

Dear Heavenly Father, send love, quench this burning hunger in my soul.

I'm not your wife, why am I so fixated to thee?

I need a strong stimulant to take this fixation from me.

Dear Heavenly Father, send love, quench this burning hunger in my soul.

The years roll by, I still feel the same.

Is there no answer, to this feeling of vain?

Dear Heavenly Father, Dear Heavenly Father, Dear Heavenly Father,

send love, quench this burning hunger in my soul.

A–men

A–men

I praise thee, I love thee

I praise thee, I love thee

A–men, A–men a–a--men

DEATH'S GUARANTEE

Oh death, that will not let me go

Is this the price for life, I have to pay?

Is there no way that I can spare? I am young,

but the thoughts my mind often crossed.

My heart, my soul, are half-decided. But often you

come, let our lives glide. Our friends, our

relatives, do not coincide. Creators' sentences
must be abided ---

even-even if we are half-decided.

A BOLD FACE

A bold face can help to save the day

It's often used to prevent dismay.

No one sees when you hurt. No one hears when
you cry.

No one feels your deepest pain.

A bold face protects internal strains.

Cry, cry, cry. Let the tears roll,

let the tears roll.

The pain, the pain can be easier to bear.

Loosen that bold face, loosen that bold face.

Give others a chance to know.

There are many who love you so.

Cry, cry, cry. Let the tears roll,

let the tears roll.

There are many who care,

Many who want to share. Your pain, your pain,

they are waiting to help you bear.

Loosen that bold face, loosen that bold face.

Cry, cry, cry. Let the tears roll,

let the tears roll.

They are still waiting to share your sorrow joy,

Hope, madness, sadness, and despair.

Loosen that bold face, loosen that bold face.

Cry, cry, cry. Let the tears roll,

let the tears roll.

suicide, suicide, suicide, the end product, of
severe excruciating pain,

dissected your body, impregnated your mind.

A leaf on a stormy night, cut frozen, blown

By the wind chill blain.

Loosen that bold face, loosen that bold face.

Cry, cry, cry. Let the tears roll,

let the tears roll.

It's your culture's pride, that women should cry,

And men should not. You are not God Almighty; do
you always have to be on top?

Just when we thought everything was well,

The announcer announced that you are dead.

Loosen that bold face, loosen that bold face.

Cry, cry, cry. Let the tears roll, let the tears roll.

THE BABY SHE WANTED, BUT COULDN'T HAVE

Poverty-stricken mind, imprisoned the baby she
wanted, but couldn't have.
Daddy is gone, he had his reason.

    The baby she wanted, but couldn't have

A mother's mind is hard to reconcile
With daddy gone, she must decide
Went to a preacher, dear Lord he prayed

    The baby she wanted, but couldn't have

Went to a psychiatrist, he diagnosed
He said, "Woman, you are not married, you must
be out of your head"

    The baby she wanted, but couldn't have

A mother's mind is hard to reconcile
With daddy gone, she must decide
No one to help her, to be by her side
A hard decision, she faces in her life

    The baby she wanted, but couldn't have

THE FORSAKEN ONES

How many years ought thou been at this place?

Long enough to watch the years and years

Spring, Summer, Winter, and Autumn, children grow

Winters deface my brows and leaves no longer show

May I say then

You are familiar with each and every face.

Tis' right my dear, tis' right dear sir.

I have observed through wrinkled brows and masked eyes

Every woman in travail.

Glistening and sparkling of christening gowns

And square-top, black graduation hats.

Their faces I have dried with apron tails

After mothers spanked and peers failed.

Now I'm old, withered, dry, and grey

Those brutalized faces, no longer look my way.

Tis' as if I'm not from here

Never acquainted with human tears.

Only the Spring, Summer, Winter, Autumn

Deface my brows, as they pass by.

2.
Phrases

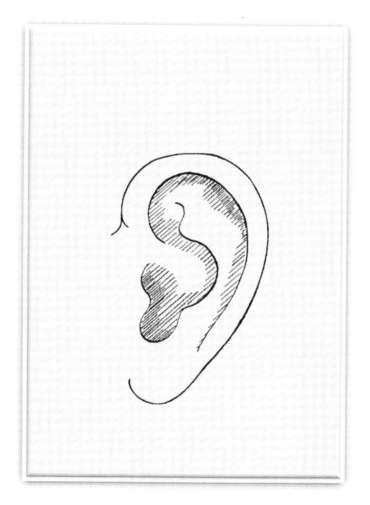

Illustration by: Hyacinth Williams-Moncrieffe

1.

A wise man thinks before he speaks
An unwise man thinks after he speaks
Later sadly dabbles in sorrow and guilt.

2.

Fogs and mists encamp my sight
All my lilies' heads bow light.
Some are hidden, what a sight,
Peeping eyes fighting bright.

3.

Each day if you motivate only
One mind encouragement of others
that's fine. One less retarded mind lags behind.

4.

Merciful father, Merciful father
                            give me time
                            give me time
                            give me time
Tomorrow, tomorrow may not be mine
            we daily trespass on borrowed time.

5.

He who thrives the highest
To the top he must excel
Bids others farewell.

6.

Boys punished when small
Mothers did you do it all?
Now men strike back all.

7.

Men bow down to pray

The moon beyond the horizon
Streams and valleys flow.

8.
Can love be defined?
It leaves confusion on
Men's minds.

9.
The brilliance of the pen in
conjunction with the mind can
make a lot of people kind or unkind.

10.
When women go to war
who will bring forth superstars?
Medically, fertility is dangerous after thirty-five.

11.
I believe in ERA. What is
Wrong with equal pay,
Equal pension, and social security?

12.
The lane you are walking in, I had been
there before. Use me as your explorer,
a romantic, experimental lover.

13.
You may love me for my money
but you won't spend a dime my honey
it's bonded in a Swiss bank account.

14.
You don't know what makes me tick

you'll be furious when I find a better chick.

15.
Your mind is as nasty as
your _____.

16.
I know you want a divorce
but I wouldn't spend a cent on you
You are of no worth.

17.
Sometimes love is unspoken
But body language can be mistaken
Tell me directly how you feel.

18.
Separation and loneliness not always fun
Admit your feelings I'll come around.

19.
I don't recall hating you
But the things you make me do
are incredible.

20.
I go crazy when I think of you
but I am afraid to let you know.

21.
There must be a reason for your behavior
Sometimes you do not know them. If you

ever found out, please let me know.

22.
Don't think you are irreplaceable
My darling
Love cannot be eaten
I'm in a depression
Start letting it on.

23.
Always absent on pay day
When you want love, you don't
Delay.

24.
Think you can find better anywhere?
I'm waiting, you will return, when you
realize it's not there.

25.
I don't drink soup when it's hot
When it's cold don't look back.

26.
Your enemy may have difficulty killing you.
Your friends know always how to hurt you.
They know many things about you.
Don't be so paranoid.

27.
You use me, I use you
We satisfy each other's needs
That's why we are compatible
So, what's the fuss all about?

28.
I got your ticket honey
When I give you a let down

You will be more than scared.

29.
We need better communications around here
I can't read your mind. I am not a fortune-teller.

3.
Love & Comfort

Illustration by: Hyacinth Williams-Moncrieffe

CAN'T LIVE WITHOUT YOU

Can't live without you
Being with you is like
The air I breathe momentarily
From day-to-day
Holding you, I absorb strength
That allows me to walk with feelings
Of supremacy. I just can't live, live
Without you.

Loving you is a balance to my equilibrium
Physically and emotionally. It is like
I have drunken a cool tiply-chilled
Glass of water on a hot day.
I just can't live, live without you.

Penetrating you is like lowering a coffin
Six feet below the ground. Deep! Deep!
Where only platy-helminthics found
I just can't live, live without you.

Walking with you vibratiously radiate feelings

Of Godliness intrinsically contrasting a
Saintly Divine by Holy Trinity.
I just can't live, live without you.

Calling you on the telephone, massively
Disseminated electrodes like a twenty-five
Millimeter gun on an Asiatic battlefield.
I just can't live, live without you.

Marrying you, a web entangled by love
Saying I do is a bond sealed with God's
Almighty kiss-balmed with aromatic per–
Fume of experience Ethiopian aged, saged-oil
I just can't live, live without you.

Having our baby, definite evidence of your
Composition. Mine! -procrastinating! Two
Human beings alive.
I just can't live, live without you.

WELCOME HOME

Welcome to my little abode
Although a temporary shelter just for few
Please make yourself at home. Home is home
Is home is home. Welcome home to my abode

And what is home? Where is home?
Home is where you feel wanted
Home is where you feel needed
Home is where you undress your mask
And naturally be yourself. Home is home
Is home is home. Welcome home to my abode

Some are so fortunate to have a home
Still others on the street they roam
When dusk arrives no place to go, they pretend
To love their friends and fellows just so that
They can be together. Home is home, is home is
Home. Welcome home to my abode

And what is home if no one cares?
And what is home with no one to share?

No dogs, no cats, no family to play
How do you spend your holiday? Maybe on your
Friend's privacy you impinge, he would be glad
Sometimes if you did not drop in. Home is home, is
home, is Home. Welcome home to my abode.

MY BLACK AFRICAN KING

Addicted to my presence, my being
like an addict to his drugs. A wino to
his wine, a faddist to his foods. Salivating juices
flow, quench your dry, hungry, thirsty soul.
You are my pedestal. You are my king, treasures
of love to your monarchy, I bring treasures of love,
gifts that no other is capable to offer. You are my
king. My Black African King.

> Sit back
> relax
> be still relax
> sh---sh–
> stretch your feet out
> let me take your slippers
> off your feet. Lavishly,
> radiantly
> anoint those toes with oil
> beneath
> You are on my pedestal. You
> are my king.
> My Black African King.

Swing from your unbalanced beams my gymnast,
swing my gymnast swing. I frequently watch you
from within. Leaching, piercing, stabbing your
neck, with vampire-like stings. Reaching the peak,
the heights, orgasmic resolution collide. Nine-
eight point six, three times ninety-eight point six
degrees, accelerated heart beats. Pumping,
escalating, rhythmic changing, ecstatic sounds, of
tachycardia. Orgasmic resolutions again collide.
Swing, swing, swing on your unbalance beams. You
are my Black African Gymnastic King.

Sit back
relax
be still relax
sh---sh–
stretch your feet out
let me take your slippers
off your feet. Lavishly,
radiantly
anoint those toes with oil
beneath
You are on my pedestal. You
are my king.
My Black African King.

Inflicted by memories of constant goose-like
touch, aphrodisiac radiation, of tongue's
saturating musk. The deep, deep pulsating of the
gluteus, contracted, rapidly. Squeeze! Squeeze!
Squeeze!----the muscular, orgasmic resolutions
again, collide, collide----ooooooooooh! The beauty,
the beauty of nature's lush. You are on my
pedestal. You are my king. Treasures to your
monarchy I bring. Gifts that no other could offer.
You are my king. My Black African King.

Sit back
relax
be still relax
sh---sh–
stretch your feet out
let me take your slippers
off your feet. Lavishly,
radiantly
anoint those toes with oil
beneath

You are on my pedestal. You
are my king.
My Black African King.

Sit back
relax
be still relax
sh---sh–
stretch your feet out. Let me take your slippers
off your feet. Lavishly, radiantly anoint those toes
with oil beneath. You are on my pedestal. You are
my king. My Black African King. Treasures, gifts of
love to your monarchy I bring. Gifts that no other
could offer. You are my king. My Black African
King.

EBONY QUEEN

She is black miss Ebony
slender figure. A palm tree
her leaves shaking gently
in the wind. Leaving her destiny
to tropical hurricane. She freely
spreads her wings. Blow tropical
Hurricane, bl–ow. See the beauty.
She is black. Miss Ebonic figure
A Queen, A Queen.

She is gentle, she is warm, her
Physical structure seems firm
Yet she blows freely in the
Wind. Others empathically
Moan for her. Thinking she is so
Fragile. She walks! She shakes! She
Speaks, making gestures with
Her eyes. A palm tree
Her leaf blowing freely in
The wind. Blows her to and fro.
See the beauty, she is black. Miss

Ebonic figure. A Queen, A Queen.

She is free like the wind
Pounding, landing softly wherever she goes.
Whispering in ears. A photographic memory
Her inscription, beauty left on everything.
Spectators watch as the wind kisses her, takes her
to and fro over mountain valleys and oceans
below. Blow tropical hurricanes, bl–ow. See the
beauty. She is black Ebonic figure
A Queen, A Queen.

SECURITY AND PEACE

The joy instills in others' hearts
Opens the gates to endless paths
Many often cannot see your views
Snares they lay to encapture you
No barriers strong enough to block your path.
The power of God disseminates it all, your name is
selected in his record.

God bless the day that you were born. Your head a
guiding angel adorned with sword of peace love
secure God bless the womb from which you were
born

Your life each birthday enriches with saving grace.
This World in turmoil man searching for peace.
Gravalicious˙ tongues hate distort the gifts you
bring
God the archeologists searches every heart
With miracles of peace, he eliminates fossils
From your path.

˙A manner that is overwhelmingly excessive, in this
case the 'tongues of hatred' (auth. Note).

THE EXCHANGE

Sharing, what do we share, a gift so precious to us?
The tense longings cannot control. Never think of
the unfold. One is only one, maybe a lonely one.
But two shares make a combination of a stronger
bond.

Caring, why do we care? To quench the need,
thirst, hunger of our desires, and satisfy what our
minds and hearts desire, whether young or old, at
the end, the physical strength retires.

Longing? Why do we long? To feel the mutual,
tender touch one missed. They plague our dreams,
they always exist. The sweet, juicy caresses of
spicy lips, anoint our faces, and our cheeks with
bliss. The chemical flows when you walk, the
energy expressed when you talk. The need to
exchange will always exist if your basic needs are
missed.

Are these the feelings of love? They excite your
mind, make it null. Everything so firmly encircled,
in a minute world. Protected from unscrupulous
hands, or something that may try to break your
bond. It must never be broken. We have already
exchanged our hands.

My everything, your everything.
My world, your world of sharing, caring.
quenching hunger, longing thirst. Carefully
sealed, by an incredible, permanent, paramount,
sacred hand. A guard of sunshine, darkness,
eternity stands. The need to exchange still exists.

No sign of human history divulged. The bed already made, will not be unmade. White shadows are undisturbed --- The exchange. The exchange, the exchange, the exchange. The exchange daily knocks at our doors.

EVENING OF SMILES

The evenings I spent in those
Environments were pleasant ones
I must consent, smiles created
radiant faces, bloomed like transparent
tablecloth, covered flowered laces.
Pedal soft my evenings in
glided places.

SITTING BY THE SHORE

Sitting by the shore watching tides roll by
The steam boats glide and the copters
fly, oh we are happy sitting by the shore.
Penguins perch, the elderlies search
picking flowers along the shore.
The tram wheels roll and cars rush by, oh
we are happy sitting by the shore.
The cold wind blows and the Autumn roars
People rush hastily in the minibus. The steam-
boats glide and the copters fly.
Oh, we are happy sitting by the shore.
Children hop and the workmen mop
Oh, we are happy sitting by the shore.
The steam-boats glide and the copters
fly, oh we are happy sitting by the shore.

NATURE KNOWS THAT THEY BELONG

Lia-MeMe and Lenox John, their bodies entwined
Expressed like one.
Soul heart and mind move sexually rhythmically in
line. Their bodies moved and shaped like one.
Lia-MeMe and Lenox John, nature knows that they
belong.
She never creates anything that's wrong.

Two artists, words timing beauty meant so much
to them.
That portrait-shapen by natures whelm. Oh–
Ebonic
Figure made to your desire, Lia-MeMe and Lenox
John
Their bodies moved and shaped like one.
Nature knows that they belong.
She never creates anything that's wrong.

Experimenters, geniuses, creators of arts, music,
dances, and poetry.
Their bodies move accurately at a rhythmic
glance,
Bring about feelings in a figurative romance.

Lia-MeMe and Lenox John, nature knows that they
belong.
She never creates anything that's wrong.

DEDICATED LADIES

Ladies of modern time, you

have taught everything in line

Thy brilliance we adore, just like Nightingale bore.

Your goals are exactly the same, motivated not to

Live in vain

Keep on dear ladies of modern time

Each life you save is counted more than once. Keep

on dear ladies of modern time.

YEARNING

Dim valleys I see when I ache for you
Like lost sheep at nights, I lay and cry
The cry I need to set me free. The cry I need to
untangle me. Lost sheep in the valley I'm aching
for you to come home.
Can't you see I'm all alone.

If by chance you care to return. My door is always
open for you. No one can ever take your place. No
one to me was ever that great. I clothed myself in
darkened robe, yearning to be on your journey or
yearning for you to return.
Please lost sheep will you return?
Can't you see I'm all alone?

THE APOLOGY

I apologize for the mistakes that I made.

I apologize for the headaches, I thought I created.

The fault not only on your behalf

I will take responsibility for my half.

I want to tell you, I will not

hurt you again. But I'm not sure if I can

I want to say the mistakes were unintended

Consciously I was not aware. But maybe sometimes

I didn't care. We have passed the slipping stage of

love my dear. A question has been plaguing my

mind and it has been for a very long time.

Where did we went wrong? And why so long we

acted as if we belong? I apologize to make things

right not wrong.

SWEET LILIES HORIZON

Sweet lilies horizon entice my brow.
Hush, hush the sound! Wind gone by the willows.
Like birds at night sleeping on my pillows.
Lying by the fountain with thy head bowed.
Sleep on beloved, sweet dreams surround now.
Regress thy footsteps from childhood mellows.
How entangled life like death's umbrellas.
Languished and weeping. Brother how art thou?
Thy journey a going right on beyond.
Caught up in thy dreams lying on the floor.
When I awakened everything was gone.
Life was even cut parallel and wrong.
All fears disappear never knock my door.
Relief with grief's fear never knocks it's strong.

ANNIVERSAY OF LOVE

The year rolled by very fast.

Winter is gone now it's spring.

It's past, It's past. It's our Anniversary.

It's our anniversary

Our anniversary of love.

I remember the month, wasn't sure of the date.

Is it the eighth or nineth? I tapped my forehead.

It's our anniversary,

Our anniversary of love.

Could you have forgotten, I thought you could not.

Ah! Ah! the three red roses, you brought on

Mother's Day. It was the eighth

The eighth of May. It's our anniversary, our

anniversary, our anniversary of love.

THE BURNT ROSE

Blaming you for burning my rose

It's often worn on evening gowns

To all important functions went

It's of little value to you

The importance of this rose you

Do not know

OUTBURST OF LOVE

I will make you love me when kissing
       tantalize you when dancing
   I'll make you love me like you
had never loved before
I will make you want me like you had
never wanted anyone before
You will forever want more
and more and more and ---More! Ooooh more.

SEASON'S GREETINGS

May these seasons bring good wishes to you
Not only today but all year through

May you prosper with good health, friendship
love, joy, hope, and peace

May the blessings today set your mind at ease
And on your face, it will show
                walking your friends will see the glow.

THANKS TO NATURE

We should be thankful for little things.

The joy each new day glory brings.

Like waking early in the morn, splashing

A little cold water on your face. Just

Hearing the soft drops from the rain,

walking barefoot on a dewy day. Playing,

running in the snow

It's such a gorgeous, beautiful, wintry day.

THE PROPELLA

It's a long time since we said goodbye.

But love's strong bond wants to fly.

A propella moving inside of me,

Emotions deserted and want to be,

Stop that propella moving, beating, inside of me.

My hours of sleep, frequently disturbed.

And body moooooved, like it had been submerged.

Those damn sweet moments, I can't forget.

The propella beating, beating,

Inside of me.

My body moved --- and twirled, and swirled,

Oh, mother's breast! I longed to get

Like a child my tongue met

The propella beats faster, faster, faster yet.

Stop that propella, that propella, propella, pella, pella

Beating, Beating, inside of me.

ADDICTION

I'm still up with the clock at dawn

Seccie and Peppie didn't work

Gosh I'm still jittery and it's still

After three

There was a "da'lin' little nurse on the

Floor last time when I woke up at two."

She gave me a shot of Seccie and Peppie

However, I can't remember her name right now.
Oh, she is so "da'lin, that da'lin' sweet little
thing."

RAIN DROPS

The rain is icy lemon drops

That decorated my double decker

Peach Carvel ice-cream cone

My tongue I use to lick the drops

They are blessings from my father's throne

My eyes blink to beckon them

Soldiers parading - bowing to my father's

command.

They platter-platter on my hat.

Those footsteps from the horses' hooves.

Faster, faster, pelted the drops like seagulls

heading to the shore,

catching fishes, angrily,

hungrily,

they hunted for more.

FRIENDSHIP

Friendship is caring for the other

Friendship is sharing time together

Friendship is feelings for your brother

Friendship is wanting to be together

Friendship can be just talking to each other

Friendship is smiling with your sister

Friendship is understanding your partner

Friendship is walking closely together

Friendship is helping when it's desired

Friendship is not necessarily agreeing with each other

Friendship is simply, truly, loving each other.

JUST FOR MOTHER A VERY SPECIAL LADY

Thank you, mother, for doing a wonderful job with
me.
One that only nature prepared you to be.
The job you were not graded for.
The job you were not rated for
With your gentle yet strong hands, mind love
touch,
You shapely molded me, a pot of clay very humbly.
Your product a functional child adjusting to
society.
Thank you, mother, for the structure you laid.
Thank you, mother, for the foundation you made.
Thank you, mother, in a very special way.

Thank you, mother, for the patience.
Thank you, mother, for your diligence.
Thank you, mother, for feeding me when I was
very hungry.
Thank you, mother, for changing me when I was
wet as a fish could be.
When there was no one else who would, when
there was no one else who could.
Thank you, mother, for truly loving me.

Thank you, mother, for bathing me when water
was unavailable
You walked many miles, stole water from a rich
white man's well.
Risked your life to be bitten by his well-trained
guard dogs.
To you that did not mean much at all.
Thank you, mother, for caring for me.
Thank you, mother, for loving me.

There is no one with whom you can compare, you
are special in many, many ways.
Thank you, mother, for loving me,
Thank you, mother, for teaching me.

Thank you, mother, for bringing me on this land.
The pains you bore I can understand.
I have children of my own, experiencing what it's
like to nurture, care for them all the while.
Although sometimes I did not treat you right,
with your courage you had put up a great fight,
saying the strongest will survive.
Thank you, mother, for giving me this life, most
times my papa was never by your side, you cared
for me, cared for me all the while.
Thank you, mother, for loving me,
Thank you, mother, for teaching me.
Thank you, mother, for caring for me.
This poem is not an apology.
It's my love, a token, a gift, for what you did.
Thank you, mother.
Thank you, mother, for loving me.
To mama: from your daughter or your son.

BACK-A-YARD

Me ti me head. Me sister seh me looking dread.
Me in America 13 years, but sometimes me still
like me niggerish ways.
Me tie me head with floral bandana spread.
Back-a-yard, me know whey me come fram
(me remembah whey me come from): JAMAICA.

It's not, it's not that ah don't like to act American.
It's just that, it's just that I like to remember whey
me come from.
When me a likkle gal yuh see?
Me carry watah pon me head an tobacco, till me
head-middle peeeel!
Yuh remembah picharie? Ah same way it stay!
Me tie me head with floral bandana spread.
Back-a-yard, me know whey me come fram:
JAMAICA.

Me know whey me come fram, yuh noe?
(Heh! Hehhh!)
(grunt) Sometimes me still like me niggerish ways.
Me tie me head with floral bandana spread.
Back-a-yard, me remembah whey me come fram:
JAMAICA.

Yuh now, yuh noe sometimes in de summer yuh
see?
Me still get di itch. Lawwwd gal, me still get di
itch!
Mi put on towerile dress, and sampata shoes.
In America?
Me tie me head, with floral bandana spread.
Me remembah whey me come fram.
Back-A-Yard!
Me seh, BACK-A-YARD! JAMAICA!

4.
Daily Nourishment

Illustration By: Denise Bryan

DAILY NOURISHMENT

I must find time to pray each day

It can be done in a simple way

A half a second one word or few

You may say, thank you Father for creating me or

even bless you for the strength.

Just these words can help to set the mind at ease.

REFUSE TO ACCEPT YOUR CULTURE'S PRIDE

Refuse to accept where you are from

Adopt the cultures of various lands

You are transformed, no longer think that

we are one, much more remember where you are from.

Refuse to accept your culture's pride

Although convinced of your culture's pride

Sometimes you even run and hide, because you

know that you are melting inside. The small voice

whispers, you are from African tribe.

Refuse to accept your culture's pride

Black fathers, Black mothers, sisters and brothers,

help to maintain your culture's pride.

Teach the young how to abide, refusing still,

refusing to accept where you are from.

You are the children of African land.

Can't you even smile with me once in a while?

I'M NOT PERFECT

I'm not perfect in everything I do

Unconsciously, sometimes, I slip a little untrue.

But is it so impractical to ask understanding of
you?

Because somethings did not come through

I am not perfect in everything I do.

Are you aware that some days my actions change?

And my kinesthetic energy is partly to blame?

All I ask is understanding of you, your borrowed

energy may help me through. I am not perfect in

everything I do.

We are not perfect in everything we do.

We make mistakes and play games too.

We may not understand some important things
said,

because your culture was misread. Sometimes I

may impinge on you. Can you imagine what I'm

 going through? I am not perfect in everything I do.

I'm not perfect in everything I do.

My misplaced artifacts may look brand new.

So often admired by people around. Did you

observe, question the ones with the slanted
frowns?

Others are treated sometimes just as unkind,

invisible scars and lesions left on their minds.

We are not perfect in everything we do -But, but

that's being a part of human too.

REALISTICALLY DELVING

There are times when I'm here
times when I'm not
searching to make
outer contacts.
Telephone rings
Doorbell chimes
but I didn't hear an earthly
line.
Delving.
Realistically delving
to know the Self.

Mind expanding
to such depth.
Expelling things
made you wept
to know that one day
man must die
Changes lift the veil
that makes you cry
Delving.

realistically delving
to know the Self.

Questions often asked by life
like who? How? Where? When?
what? And why?
Give me a puzzle
let me try
searching
collecting answers
to satisfy
life's questions that's why
Delving.
realistically delving
to know the Self.

THE PROTECTION

Building mountains!
to protect your mind
but strong winds came
and down they twirl
Mother Nature,
Mother nature cannot be
unfurled.

Building fences!
To protect your land
on your ground your neighbors
cannot stand
but heavy rains came
down upon the land
Mother Nature,
Mother nature we must
understand.

Building barriers!
to protect your mind
but the spiritual forces

penetrate your lines
Almighty God, Creator
        Greater than mankind!
Mother Nature,
            Mother Nature always on
                                time.

Covering your beauty
that it cannot be seen
put on veils, crocus or
                        gabardine
but a radiant portrait
is unmistakably seen
Mother Nature,
        Mother Nature daintily
                created a queen.

BROOKLYN

In Brooklyn a variety of trees grow
People sit on carved benches along the
Roads, enjoying the coolness of the park's
Summer breeze. June brides fulfilling their
Fantasy dreams, strolling with grooms their
Hands buckled while enjoying the scenes.
Brooklyn, Brooklyn, Brooklyn a place for you and
me.

In Brooklyn where landscapes lie, I wish
They were aligned by grandiose mountains
Touching the sky. But I see the peeks of
High rise buildings and churches instead.
Still many things for Brooklyn can be said
Brooklyn, Brooklyn, Brooklyn a place for you and
me.

He rises early in the morn gormandizingly
brushing
The outline of the dawn, painted the rising Sun.
Artists with eagle and brush capturing
The beauty of mother nature's lush, hung the
pieces
On museum walls so that your generation and
mine
Can enjoy. Brooklyn, Brooklyn, Brooklyn a place
for you and me.
Brooklyn's a home where famous people are from,
poets
Leaders philosophers academicians and a mother
of
Many movie-stars. She leaves her marks near and
far

Brooklyn, oh, she is unpredictable as the spring
forecast
Yet wee beauty when we pass. Brownstone
Houses, cottages. Mansions.
Brooklyn, Brooklyn, Brooklyn a place for you and
me.

Brooklyn's a place for everyone.
She's filled with madness and fun.
Some big-shots own yachts, while some small-
shots cuddle in zero-degree weather, in
abandoned buildings, like frozen rats. Still others
wear expensive clothes, while others shop in the
Salvation Army's, second-hand store. The
have/the haves not,
They always want more, the have nots' left with a
zero score.
Yet Brooklyn maintains her beauty. She is proud,
unpredictable,
She is madness, she is sadness, like other places
and towns.
Brooklyn, Brooklyn, Brooklyn a place for
everyone.
A place for me and for you.

SITTING PRETTY

Sitting pretty, legs crisscrossed, pillows at your
head.

I am thinking more than you at that

said moment how to be better than you

At your lovely moments I'll conquer you

     sitting pretty, sitting pretty, legs crisscrossed

        below your knee.

Conflicts you are forced to create

ulterior forces sharpening weapons to under-

mine your estate. I think just like you

but I want to be better than you. In your

loneliest moments I will conquer you

     sitting pretty, sitting pretty, legs crisscrossed

        only below your knee.

EVERYONE HAS A TALENT

Everyone has a talent

It may not be like your friends or mine

Often your talent is sat upon

Why worry about mine and everyone's?

Exert your strength, mind, hands,

An unused talent will be trodden on.

BENEATH THE OCEAN'S BED

If the sea could only say
Waters roll from where they lay
You and I would be surprised of
Things beneath the ocean's bed

Muggers use, discard their preys
Murder weapons in it laid. Hidden
Jewels and treasures stayed pedestrians'
Garbage dumped like clay. Come with me
Take a dive! You and I will be surprised
Of things beneath the ocean's bed

MAN WILL ALWAYS BE HERE

So many images shaped on doors

insignias inscriptions on institutions galore.

Man wants his presence to be always here

afraid not hearing he was never here

Fixation seen in baby-like stage.

The blanket that covers painful days.

Achieving knowledge wealth to be on top

The biological wheel lets it take a flop.

No longer knowing, seeing, hearing,

Whose footsteps trot.

Refraining not to argue with my king

For all the creativity he makes me bring

Now excluded me from his throne

Practicality makes room for young seeds to be
sown.

A generative degenerative cycle takes its turn.

A wheel in motion-combustion watches the
catalyst as it burns.

Life cycle turns, and turns, and turns, and turns.

BORROWED LOVE

Lady when are you going to get a man of your own,
someone who you can adore? Someone who
respects you. Someone who loves you. Enlighten
your mind. How long does it take for you to know
borrowed love, borrowed love is never sure?

Lady when are you going to get a man of your own?
You have been waiting, waiting for that train too
long. In a station it may never come. You feel
rejected, humiliated, unwanted. A piece of
garbage rejected by all trash cans. There is no
wastebasket in which you can lie much more to
stand. Lady get yourself another man. This one
belongs to someone. Borrowed love, borrowed
love, borrowed love is never sure.

In the mirror you hardly look. Infrequently you
take a partial glance or two. You should be looking
in it more. Your beautiful face used to shoe.
Enlighten your mind. A borrowed love is never
sure. On your lapel, the lapel is called the devil's
whore.

It's a pity you no longer smile. Driven to insanity,
laden with perplexities. You are an empty casket,
rejected by the Dead. Degenerative husk remained
where it laid. Powerless ever it is to rise. Rise, rise,
rise ---, do not sleep forever. Once you had a mind,
a mind of your own. But don't you have it
anymore, a borrowed love is never sure. The label
on your lapel is called the devil's whore.

Lady when are you going to get a man of your own,
own that you can adore? A new formation under
your skin, changed the pigmentation within. The
bitterness secretes, discolors the outer skin. The

indescribable mixtures of hormones combined infectious toxins allergize and saturate your mind. Metastasis of carbuncles desecrate the interior radiates, constantly radiates to the exterior. A mirror you don't look in anymore, borrowed love, borrowed love is never sure. Your label on your lapel is called the devil's whore.

Lady when are you going to get a man of your own, someone that you can adore? You are maggot infested. You are even constipated. Bitter, bitter, bitter inside. One-Hundred and eighty centiliters of black and white may not help you. Flushed with five thousand centiliters of SSE. This still cannot touch you. Lady, you need to be cleansed I pray that the Holy Ghost touch your soul. Why don't you get someone of your own, a borrowed love is never sure?

What do you plan to do, kill the man's wife? What are you waiting for, for her to die? She is healthy, she is young, you will be two times waiting very long. What's your next plan to commit suicide? Lady, your train will never pass by. Get someone who loves you. Get someone who respects you. Get someone who adores you. You have been waiting for this unavailable man. Borrowed love, borrowed love, borrowed love, is never sure.

DO YOU KNOW THE TRUE ME?

Wanting me for what I am
Surprised later to know who I am
Do you know the true me?
On several occasions we met
displayed unique professional traits not once did
you find time to ask, to observe the true me.

If geniusity is craziness, profoundly classified as
abnormalcy then, then there is a wide spectrum of
pathology, floating around in society, wanting me
for what I am. Surprised later to know who I am,
do you know the true me?

A creative mind unpredictable all the time. It's a
long-drawn line to infinity. Geniuses create
laughter complex simple structured forms, an
essential foundation of earthly lawns. Mankind
hates, loves, abhors, enjoys what geniuses find.
Wanting me for what I am. Are you surprised later
to know who I am? Do you really know the true me?

There are many, many restless minds, searching
the environment all the time. Sometimes living in
a world of fantasy, extract from it reality.
Explicably they draw from dreams create the
nucleus of modern technology. Man, man creates
a new world from fantasy. Warning me for what I
am, surprised later to know who I am. Do you
really know the true me?

If there is a creator, a hell a heaven, a selected
judgment day, and sentences, sentences are the
prices we have to pay.

They must be allocated equally instead of stereotypically. Geniuses come in all shapes, forms, their creativity, a gift with it, they were born. Mankind loves, hates, abhors, what geniuses find. Habitating Rembrandts of their history in expensive vaults as you can see.

If I cannot be a genius myself, then I will hold on to an autograph; his wealth, history, and treasures, that are my desire, wanting me for what I am. Surprised later to know who I am. Do you intend, can you find time to know the true me?

ANALOGY OF A CHILD

Does a mother truly know her child?
Does a father truly know his child?
Does a child truly know his child?
Many things to him are blind. A mask worn, so
many things it hides.
The secret parts no one sees. The closed parts no
one knows.
Yet the open part is shown, a mask used to
perform brilliant shows.
Hurry! Find the etiology that no one knows.
A door is locked, a key is thrown.

The hurts suffered in early years can mature later
to hatred. Propelling the adult, a woman, a man,
searching restlessly for something to hold on.
Sometimes many may say, yet depart without
saying good day. So many things affecting life: A
battered child, a hungry child, a labeled child, an
unloved child, an unwanted child. Needing more,
demanding more. This unsatisfied mixture
comprised society. How many still needing,
wanting more?
Sibling rivalry, don't call it love
Sibling rivalry don't call it pride
Sibling rivalry can destroy family ties.
The insecurity increases, increases inside
Jealousy displayed on your bride
Even close friends by your side
Hurry-Hurry, find the etiology that eats the inside.

Children abhor parents at times, when inhibiting
their pleasuring minds. Sometimes they are glad
for their descent. A compensating gift they send.

Saturating parents with guilty confessions.
Languish, yearning to be loved, to be touched, to
be hugged, to be kissed. Languish, yearning if it's

even to be two feet from their side. Hurry! Find
the etiology that eats the inside.

Performing my duty, a child may say. It's
acknowledged by the world in many ways. Who
are they, expecting so much of you? Who are they
observing you? Three generations, preachers,
teachers, peers, members of communities. When
you satisfy their minds, you don't have to ask.
Bravo, bravo, the claps rung fast. If and when they
are displeased, angry eyes, from them are seen.
Hurry! Find the etiology that eats the inside.

Can anyone understand?
Can anyone see it my way?
Yes, we can see the heart, how it reacts to stressful
thoughts. But worst of all we cannot see the mind
it possesses, hypothetical signs. Dormantly things
are so blind. Does a mother know her child? Does a
father know his child? Hurry! Find the etiology
that eats the inside.

Exerting cleverly by the slip of tongue.
How it makes a lot of people dumbfound.
Dreams erode, cleansing souls in depth.
Rebuke the enemies who transgress.
Intrinsically our minds are possessed.
Only assume you know your child, since you
correlate with him once in a while. Incestingly
how children play, harbored hatred all the way.
Those angry ties suppressed, emerged
spontaneously by a simple test. Does a mother
know her child? Does a father know his child?
Hurry! Find the etiology that eats the inside.

GUILT'S COMPENSATION

You cannot bring the dead back from the grave. Too late to compensate for mistakes you thought you had made. Remembering when loved ones speak angrily with you, explained you are a resident here not an alien, new. Maybe they did not agree with you. But are you still pleading for their excuse? Stop compensating for mistakes you thought, you had made. Your loved ones resting peacefully in the grave.

Living each day in sublime, cautiously answering questions all the time. Fearing to make another mistake. You are human, that's your place. Dear ones visiting Destiny Land. Are you still hoarding a guilty mind? Smiling, laughing all the time, just to keep it from everyone.

They are dissected by a physical detachment stone. Each day on your mind they atone. Stop compensating for mistakes you thought you had made. Your loved ones resting peacefully in the grave.

THE ESCAPE FROM INSANITY

Peace, peace, silent moments of peace
Unhurried, uninvited tranquil moments of excess
serenity
No one with whom thoughts can be shared
No one with whom to sit very near
Peace, love, joy, hope, hours
of tranquility, searching for a road not leading to
insanity.

The walls of bedrooms, living rooms all the rooms
in the house are very expensively. Awards,
paintings by Picasso, sculptures and pictures of the
Mona Lisa. I have accumulated everything the
hearts of men dire. But still lonely moments my
footsteps make. I have covered, shampooed the
variegated Persian rug, with a million steps of
anxiety. The wood in the fireplace burning,
burning bright. Red flames flicker clapping many
lights. Still, still my body lurks giant iceberg
inside. Searching for peace, love, joy, hope, hours
of tranquility escaping from moments of insanity.

Peace, peace silent moments of peace. Those damn
achievements symbols on the walls pierced my
eyes constantly. Maybe I'll feel better if I listen to
the melodic sounds of operatic music. Maybe twist
my body to rockers and disco beats. Maybe I'll
recite some poetry, Shakespeare's, Browning's,
Poe's Poe, yes, yes, Alan Poe, or watch television,
watch a good-good-good old show. Perhaps look at
Cable, something sexy should be on this late, late
time of the night. Got to have peace, peace silent
moments of unhurried or invited peace. The whole

damn world seems to be crushing, crushing, crushing down on me. The whole damn world seems to be moving, moving, moving, in, in, in me.

Peace, peace silent moments of peace. No one with whom to share your thoughts. Not another human being to admire while sleep. Everything seems frozen, empty, the iceberg still lurks inside. Yet, yet the wood in the fireplace burns very, very bright. Oh no --- forget about all this nonsense. I can, I can, I can go to my bed. I will sleep like a log tonight. On the other hand, I think, I think I better not tonight unless I drink something instead. Something, something strong, very strong. Yes, yes, the concentrated strength of a special exotic dessert wine. Something stronger to eliminate the sad, dark, pale, cold moments from my mind. The whole world seems, seems to be crushing, crushing, moving, moving, in on me. I need an escape from insanity.

Peace, peace, moments of unhurried, uninvited peace, constantly, constantly plaguing my mind. Constantly, constantly controls my life. Yes, yes, I need to hang loose in a state of euphoria. I can see the monkey swinging in the forest, from tree-to-tree, limb-to-limb, branches-to-branches. Look at me, just look at me. That is where I'd rather be.

Yes, yes, drugs, drugs, the answer to all my sorrows, to all my problems. That's where I would rather be free from pain and reality. Peace, peace, love, joy, hope, searching for an escape from insanity.

As high as a kite above mountains, I will fly. Propelled by the wind, I will rock and rock, over deserts, valleys, or mountain-tops. No trace, no remembrance of peace that is uninvited, unhurried, that seems to be crushing, crushing, in, in, in on me. No trace of unhurried, uninvited peace that momently moves, moves, moves down, down, down, down on me. That's the place I'd rather be. A place that is refuge from insanity.

Peace, peace, searching for moments of unhurried or uninvited peace, peace, peace, searching for love, joy, hope, moments of true serenity. But still, still in my dreams, I experience them. Still in my dreams, the figures of bleak, pale, black, creatures cry, searching, searching for true tranquility. No providence of any escape from insanity.

I have spent enough money purchasing young lovers. In my village, I am famous as a baby killer. I have worn the most expensive clothes, taken the most expensive trips offered. Engrossed in some of the most hazardous sports, yet, yet I am unable to truly find what my heart and mind desire. Peace, peace, true peace, love, joy, hope, permanent moments of wanted, invited tranquility. To be

close by another. To smell the fresh aroma of body
odor. I guess I will be searching, searching,
searching yonder forever and ever, and ever, and
ever yonder --- yonder --- yonder forever,
escaping from - the–world -to - insanity.

THREE MUGS ON A SHELF

Three mugs on a shelf, one blue, one silvery, one white, all have initials. Could they be–long to the two ladies and a gentleman sitting at the three desks. Three mugs they are sit–ting on a shelf.

The big mug has a "B", the small mug has a "B", the largest mug a "W." Two ladies white, the gentleman black, with three mugs on a shelf, what's the meaning of that? Who among the three is on top? Three mugs on a shelf, just sitting like that.

Water taken from the fountain; everyone had their drink. They used sanitary cups, dumped them in one direct spot. The mugs were still on the shelf sit-ting in their spots. Three mugs on a shelf, what is the meaning of that?

The gentle man sat just spinning in his chair.

He seemed unaware of his environment. He was not aware that I was even there. Three mugs a on a shelf just sitting in their spots. Three mugs on a shelf, what is the meaning of that?

MESSAGE FROM YOUR PRESIDENT

This place is going to be in a storm
The President predicted as he forewarned
People did not heed to his rules
They also called father Noah a fool

Months and months it went by
But they still did not heed
To his cry. They all thought
He was telling a lie

There is a gas shortage in sight
But still no one even replied
We are spending beyond our means
Other countries getting rich at
Our expense it seems

This old bean head many said
He is going senile instead
The lines are long at the pump

Waiting to be filled they honk
And honk. Lips dropped, face masked,
Some used this excuse to pull their tasks.

United States my second country, to me it is a
mighty land. If she loses all her values, she will be
unable to stand. Citizens, citizens help maintain
your country's brand.

When you're strong, you have lots of friends
When you are weak, they all descend
Listen, listen to the message from your president.

THE EXISTENCE AND THE NONEXISTENCE

Absent before the present, the existence
And the nonexistence. A creation of you a Creation
of me, controlled by chemistry
Concepts, values and prototypes.

Primitive statues replicated each new life
The nonexistence and the existence live in unison
contradictory. No warrants no contracts for us to
sign. Unnecessary to put your signature or mine.
Man's life destiny is a priori.

LIFE'S DESTINY

Sometimes beneath the waters

low

Other times above the waters

glow

So is life from day-to-day

Some may laugh and some may pray

But life owes each and every one a frown

The rich, the poor, the white, the black,

The large, the small, the skinny, the tall,

Life holds a pack for us all

It's a race that man must run.

Life's destiny rewards every man a crown.

TIME

Time, time can't hold onto time.
Running here, running there
Must get everything done in a hurry
Time, time escaping rapidly, flying
passing by you and me.

Time, time can't hold onto time.
Punching time-cards, signing records
Must get the right job, must have children now,
must get married, must lay a foundation for future
generation. My name must live forever, I am
breathless unable to speak slowly. Time, time
escaping rapidly, flying by you and me.

Time, time can't hold onto time.
It has great affects on you and me.
Hustling to catch a bus, car, a train, a plane.
Our destinations, we must be on time.
Time, time escaping rapidly, flying by you and me.

Time, time can't hold onto time. The lines on my

face, tell me very slowly, my ago no longer what I think it should be. The bones in my body are hurting arthritically. My mind is still intact. It is functioning logically. You know, I know, we can't hold onto time. It is the author, the creator, the master, a manipulator, a daily tantalizer of you and me. Time, time, time, controls our destiny. It bids goodbye to you and me.

CHARMING ANIMALS

Vicious charming animals, go to
steal the hearts of innocent women, with great
zeal. When their goals, they ascertain, they even
depart, and take their names, leaving the victims,
bathing in sorrow, shame, and pain.

To the scene of the crime, periodically, they
return to plunge a sword, into a wound. A wound
that is only half-healed. Do they not care, what
pains they inflict? Their minds are satisfied by
nasty, ugly tricks. A vicious, charming animal,
will ALWAYS steal the hearts of innocent Women,
with great zeal.

RECESSION

Often whites could not see the black man's plight.

They were living on a street called delight.

The recession now takes a toll.

Whites as well as blacks,

now dance rock and roll.

WOMAN IN TREVAIL

Enchanted by music, flashing psychedelic lights, moving circular in motion to bent love lyrics and rocking music of disco beats. The first time I saw you I wanted you. The first time I held you I needed you. Your piercing eyes caught not just a glimpse of me. They ultrasonically illustrated over my body showing endless portion of my physical structure. You said you loved me, you said you'd love me forever.

Your eyes piercing burning fire. Red red-hot flaming Sahara Desert reflecting the midday sun. Your tongue cool then warm melting mucoid volcanic lava alternately bathes my body. Your body, my body, heated by one another. Wanting, wanting each other from the start. We were destined from the beginning of time. Mind, heart intertwine. Wanting, wanting each other all the time, all the while. I love you forever. I love you forever.

Impregnated by your seed, Forty-six chromosomes of you and me. I'm carrying your baby, a special part of you and a special part of me. Brings changes in my emotions. No longer do I feel I love you. No longer do I feel you love me. No longer do I want to adore you. No longer do I want to be kissed by your cool warm mucoid tropical volcanic tongue that spills lava, lava. No longer do I feel I love you forever.

Seeing the full-erected nipples of my bosom. Seeing my protruding stomach, face covered by mask of pregnancy. No longer do you adore me. No longer do you look into my eyes. No longer do your eyes burn for me. No longer do you want to hug and kiss me. Abstain from home from me and your unborn child for days it seems forever. I wonder if you still love me, my brother, I wonder if I still love you forever?

I pray for our baby to be born, every day, each night, each morn. In the ninth month of pregnancy, you were gone. Only found out when I awakened one morn. I saw socks with cut-out toes. Your half-bleached blue-jeans left in your drawer. You left early in the morn without saying a word or bidding goodbye. No farewell given to me or your unborn child one you may never see. You left early, early like a thief in the morn. Do you still love me forever?

I cry, I mourn, I weep, my laughter mixed with tears. I pray, I cry, I cry, I pray, you were gone. Nowhere to be found. I should have hated you. I should have cursed you. But I found myself loving, loving you. Maybe because I am carrying your child. A part of you. I wonder, are you gone forever. I still love you, my brother.

Two babies wrapped in brown paper bags; umbilical cords still attached. Left in a half broken-down shack for passerby to hear them cry, for passerby to hear them moan. For passerby to hear them groan. Whimpering little hopeless children, little whimpering harmless animals all alone. Rescue, rescue my babies that I have abandoned. Where are you, my brother, the time when I need you the most? The time you can never be found. You have left me to suffer, I should have hated you, but for some strange reason I still love you. I feel I love you forever. In the ninth month of pregnancy, you left me with your two unborn children to suffer.

I felt the sensation of hot water gushing down my legs. Seeing blood streaks bright color red responding to aching pains in the lower quadrant of my back clashed with others in lower abdominopelvic area. I called your name. I see you like stars in my vision. Those same psychedelic lights flashing by. I wanted you then. I want you now forever. Wanting to be held by you. Wanting to be touched by you. Wanting to hear your voice. Wanting you to make love to me. To hear you say everything gonna be alright. Where ever you are you cannot be found; we have searched all around. In the ninth month of pregnancy, you left me. I want you now more than ever. I should have hated you. But I found myself loving sometimes it seems forever. Where are you gone, my brother?

The intolerable pains that I must bear, grinding teeth clenching fists holding hand to wooden leg of a kitchen table. The other, holding the heads of bulging babies from off dirty concrete floors. Bringing your baby, our baby into a world of poverty. Where were you when I needed you? My son, my daughter, why should they suffer? I need you. I want you. I hate you; I love you more than ever. Where are you? I call your name, John, John, John, over and over and over. I need you. I need you. I need you now more than ever. Still wanting, wanting you to make love to me, just hold me, my brother. Just to hear you say everything gonna be alright.

I should hate you, yet I love you. Why, why I wonder? Why aren't you at my side, protecting the babies we made together? You call me your woman, your sister, your babies' mother, your lover, yet you left me to suffer. Carrying, having to raise babies all alone. You have left me to suffer, you have been giving yourself to many others, I should have hated you, but I found myself loving you. I wonder why, why I even bother. I think I will love you forever.

One calamity is over, I'm faced with another. Two babies without a father. The landlord knocking kicking, he needs rent, must have it now. The last was paid I have no more. Why, why do you leave me to suffer? Those horrible moments you put me through. I want to hate you, I found myself loving you. In my womb, your seed was grown. I love you; I hate you. Why do I feel this way I wonder? You have left me with your two unborn children to suffer. In the ninth month of pregnancy when I needed you most. In the ninth month of pregnancy when we should have been close. You have left me with your children to suffer.

I wanted to hear you say everything gonna be alright. I wanted you to wipe the tears from my eyes. I wanted you to help me make decisions. Your children I no longer want to see, twenty-four hours per day they look at me. If I could only see you. If I could only hear you; just to say a word to me, my brother. Just to hear you say everything gonna be alright. Nowhere can you be found. My brother and sister have looked around. I hate you; I love you, I'm not sure what I feel for you. Why, why, why my brother, why have you left me in the ninth month of pregnancy? Left me and your two unborn children to suffer.

133

It's not your baby. It's not my bay. It's our babies. A special part of you, a special part of me. A combination of yours and my genes, forty-six chromosomes all together. Why, my brother? Wy have you left us to suffer? Why all this burden is left on me? You are running, running around free. Looking for another womb another seed to be sown. Another woman to be treated just like me. Why, my brother, don't you have any sympathy, any emotions, any feelings. Don't you hurt, don't you ache, don't you cry? Do you always lie in a catatonic state? In the ninth month of pregnancy, you walked out on me. Your face, I have not seen anymore. Your touches those memories I still adore. The decisions everything left on me. A decision to destroy, or not to destroy two human beings. The decision to be called a wicked mother. The decision to be classified as an unloved mother. A decision to be called a baby killer. Did anyone ask what's the matter? Did anyone label the father, the man who left me to suffer? Double standards double standards blared by society. In the ninth month of pregnancy, you abandon me. In the ninth month of pregnancy my face you no longer want to see. Why, why have you left me to suffer? I should have hated you, but still, I love you. Sometimes I feel it will be forever.

The same day the babies were plucked from my womb, you married another, why so soon? You have sold my blood, your blood, your generations blood, my generations blood for a few meager menial dollars. Just to maintain your fantasy fair of lying on a canopy bed instead of a Kia mattress. In the ninth month of pregnancy, you abandoned me, your two unborn children, you left us to suffer. Why, why, why my brother? I should have hated you but sometimes I feel I will love you forever.

Shame, disgust, guilt, humility flooded my mind. What did I do that was so unkind? You have left in the ninth month of pregnancy. At the time that I needed you the most. At the time that we should have been so very close. A special part of me. Two naked bodies made love, bring forth children together, that only will be cared for by one not the other. Each little child needs a father. Why, why have you abandoned us, my brother? In the ninth month of pregnancy, you left us to suffer.

three times ninety-eight-point six degree no longer burns. A womb a seed in it is sown. A seed in it is grown. A special part of you growing in me. During nine months of pregnancy. I feel the turns, a little baby for its father it yearns. I feel the kicks sometimes they are stiff, left right, left right, left right left. Why have you left me, my brother? In the ninth month of pregnancy to someone else you turn. I should have hated you, but intrinsically I was born good, I must be sweet. I must be calm. I was too loving. Is that why with me you did not stay but instead you went away? I can't stop! Won't stop, loving you. Maybe because in me special seeds for you were sown. Maybe because in me, your children have grown. I still love you my brother, although in the ninth month of pregnancy you left me and your two unborn children to suffer. Why, why, why I still ask the questions, my brother? I should have hated you. But I love you. I guess we are part of each other.

Why, why, why my brother, in the ninth month of pregnancy, you left me to suffer? You have taken everything from me. My breath, my mind, my heart, my soul, I am a bare skeleton, a mannequin in a showcase whose husk is just dressed up. When the clothes are taken off there still is nothing left. No longer do I know how to care, how to feel, how to want, how to give or how to love. Why, why, why, my brother? I'm unable to love any other. You have taken everything from me You have left me and your two unborn children in the ninth month of pregnancy to suffer. Why, why, my brother?

QUESTIONS

Am I happy to be who I am?

Am I proud of what I am?

Am I afraid to be this kind of human?

Do I prefer to be another man?

Do I ask where I am from?

Will I always live according to the will of other men?

What will be the consequences if I deviate from their plans?

Can I ever be myself?

Will I ever be myself?

Will I be deprived of the opportunity to develop my true potential?

Will I bae able to identify my roots, the place where I am from, the culture for which I longed?

A child with a mind of his own, admires beauty that he adorns

Getting praises for the seeds that he had sown.

Am I happy to be who I am?

Am I proud of what I am?

A product, a product of Nature's Hand.

CHANGING MISTAKES

So many mistakes in life we have made

So many footsteps in life we have laid

So many miles in life we have trodden

If we could turn the hands of time

Those mistakes would never be yours or mine.

Those footsteps would not have laid and those

miles would not have been trodden.

Consciously, unconsciously they bring the past,

 affect the present and the future.

Is it worthwhile to measure mistakes forever?

Is it worthwhile trying to unmake footsteps,

forever, that were laid when you did not know
better?

Is it wise to untrod miles that youth did not plan?

Things that you were not equipped to know, now

 from them you learn and grow.

THE EXECUTIONER

Who is the executioner?

Who should be sentenced?

Who is the executed?

Who are the lawmakers, by whose laws the
executer is executed?

For what reason the executioner is sentenced

Who are the murderers?

Who are passive or blood-thirsty killers?

Who are the sane?

Who judge the insane?

Who is humane?

Who is inhumane?

Who is moralistic?

Who is immoral?

Who is immortal?

Who are the jurors who sentenced the murderers?

Who is the legal executioner who injected the
lethal dose?

Passively snatch the life of the murderer, the
illegal executioner

Who is sane?

Who is insane?

For what reason was the insane sentenced

For what reason was the insane executed

Who are they who insist that the price of life the executer must pay?

Who is immortal?

Who gave life to man?

Who took life from man?

Who made the decision who should live?

Who made the decision who should die?

Who are the sane?

Who are the insane?

Who is humane?

Who is in humane?

Who is moral?

Who is immoral?

Who is immortal?

Who is mortal?

Who should be sentenced?

Who should be executed?

For what reason was the executer sentenced

For what reason did the executioner execute his victim

Who is sane?

Who is insane?

Who is moral?

Who is immoral?

Who is humane?

Who is inhumane?

Could all, all, all be the same

Moral immoral

Mortal immortal

All, all, all are all executioners the same passive or aggressive blood-thirsty killers.

ONLY TWO STEPS OVER PLEASE

You tied me down! You tied me down!

Chains. Chain. Iron chains.

Heavy, pledget, rigid, rusty

compact iron chains.

What did I di–ooh! oooh!

two steps over please.

That's all I want to go.

Whip lashing my back

blood squirted over me

Pledget chains. Pledget chains

melted my mind again.

God help me! help me!

help me please!

Blood gushed out of my mouth–

thick, crusty, giant,

iceberg-like blood

covered teeth

that were once pretty white.

Chains. Chains. Iron chains.

Only two steps over please.

That's all I want to go.

Lord God! help! help!

Only want to go

two steps over please.

Mama told me you, you're my Daddy. Move up
faster!

Iron chains

again pelted my mind.

Everything so mixed up

glistening, dazzling like

a hot sun

penetrating on fresh asphalt

melted on country roads

leaving air bubble imprints

on barefooted children.

Only two steps over please.

That's all I want to go.

Harder! harder! my feet only

reach on the same stairs.

Sweat in my eyes, swollen, red and bulged.

But-I-must-see-the-pages
around lighted firewood,
candlelight, lighted corn-stick
and Pepsi Cola goose-neck
bottle-neck lamps.
Chains! Chains! Iron chains.
Only two steps over please.
That's all I want to go.

I heard voice. Voices!
beyond those stairs.
yonder! yonder!
where it's not bare.
Green, green grass
clear brooks
crystal waters flow
from them
the affluent drink and grow.
Whoosh! Whoosh! Thank God
I'm over.
My guts, my intestines sticking out

from where it comes?

I think it was night

Accidentally got out of my sight.

Chains! Chains! Iron chains!

Only two steps over please.

That's all I want to go.

THE CALLIING

I heard the sea roar
Lightning thunderous clapping hands
The mountains shook rivers and brooks
Earthquake crackled engulfing beautiful
Shores yet the hearts of men hardened more
Might be a signal a non-verbal cue
A message relaying for me and you
The communication is coming through

MESSAGES THAT MUST BE DELIVERED TO ALL PATRIOTS AND LEADERS OF MY PEOPLE

Messages, messages not if but will and must be delivered. Messages maybe obstructed by evil hands, evil minds, sabotaging your plans only temporarily. Not necessarily by your enemies, but definitely by your friends who know our plans. Evil hands, evil minds do not need deliverance, constantly fighting to prevent interruption. Afraid to expose their tense blood thirst killer instinctuous needs. They must shine must be shown to everyone. That they are the sabotagers of plans. Messengers must deliver messages. The words must be heard. Messengers must deliver messages. The words must be heard. The children must be led. Messengers must be protected from evil hands, evil minds that interrupt plans. They will be protected by someone mightier, greater, stronger, more powerful than any other. He is the Creator whose messages you must, you will, you are called to deliver. Messages, messages, messages of a higher order.

The gifts you receive are unique ones. The messages that you must deliver are diplomatic ones. You are he special ambassador chosen to deliver my children from enemies' hands. The messages must be delivered. The words must be heard, his people must be delivered from false accusers, assassinators, hungry blood-thirsty passive killers. The messages must be delivered...Your life might be the cost. The price so many have paid. Your friends, your relatives asked is this how your Creator saves. And your enemies also laugh your energy has been taken away. Your life is a free gift given to you by the Creator. Given to you not forever. Those messages, those messages you must not if but we deliver. Messages, messages, messages given by a higher order. Those messages must be delivered.

Messages, messages that must be delivered, with or without a price a cost a fee. His words must be heard, his children must be led, your people from bondage. His words must be heard universally. Those messages must be delivered. Your life might be the cost the price you have to pay protecting the blood of many who they try to betray. Protecting future generations to come, forever your species will be around. Evil minds, evil hands will try to sabotage your plans but the messages, the messages must be delivered. There is no one mightier, greater, stronger more powerful than the Creator, whose messages, messages you must deliver. Messages, messages of a higher order. Those messages must delivered.

Messages, messages, not if but will and must be delivered. They maybe obstructed only temporarily by evil hands, evil minds trying to undermine your plans. You can be sure your friends can understand, they come in many classifications. Good friends half good friends, envious friends, zealous friends, communicative friends and only friends. Whatever their classification they serve their purposes. Friends are friends are only friends. Messages, messages you must deliver. They can only obstruct them temporarily. There is no one mightier, greater, stronger more powerful than the Creator whose messages you are sent to deliver. Messages,

messages, messages of a higher order, messages not if, you will and must deliver.

Messages, messages not if but will and must deliver. With or without a price a cost a fee, you must be ready for your journey with or without clothes, transportation, your destination you may go. Those messages must be delivered. The words must be heard, they must be spread universally. My work they might even try to credit to someone else, because I'm a threat to their health, financial wealth. I am an ambassador called by the Creator, his messages I must deliver. A star destined to travel the universe, one that shines, one that is a model for all mankind. One that forever his name will be called one that forever powerful voice we will recall. Marcus, Frederick, Malcolm, Harriett, Rosa, Marley, Martin Luther. Messages, messages they were sent to deliver.

Their names, their names my people will always remember. Their voices in their minds will always tremble. Messages, messages they were sent to deliver. Their lives, their pride was the cost many paid. Protecting your blood, my blood of future generations to follow. Your species will always be round your children will again wear their crowns. Messages, messages you must deliver. Messages, messages of a higher order. These are the messages special ambassadors must deliver.

Messages, messages you must and will deliver. The gift you bring it's a special one. You are a child of the universe from different line, lineage Kings and Queens. The fruits from their trees are also special wine from extraordinary vintages.

Messages, messages you must deliver. Judas sold Jesus for forty pieces of silver. The Blackman sold his brothers for slavery dollars. For the rest of their lives, they are trying to recover their manes their pride their dignity, culture and wealth. Messages, messages must be delivered. Messages, messages they are of a higher order. They must be delivered.

Messages, messages, messages not if but will and must be delivered We live in a so-called world of modern technology, but our hearts sometimes are as primitive as can be. W sell our brothers, sell our sisters, sell our mothers, sell our neighbors just for few capitalistic dollars. The hearts of men seem so corrupt how many of them can we trust, we have lost love now we only lust. Messages, messages, messages must be delivered. Obstructions placed temporarily in your way. They will be removed early today. But sit not back for miracles to be wrought, you must fight with all your heart. And his name we ascertain calling, calling him not in vain. There is no one mightier, greater, stronger, more powerful than the Creator whose messages you must deliver. Your life might be the price you have to pay. Many may say, many may ask is this how the Creator saves, but messages, messages must be delivered. Your life is a temporary gift to you. The Creator uses it in whatsoever way he choose. Messages, messages, messages must be

150

delivered. Messages, messages, messages of a higher order. These messages must be delivered.

WAKE UP

Are you ready America?
Are you ready my black brothers?
Are you ready my black sisters?
Tell me white America, should I
classify you as my neighbor.
Are you ready for black presidency?
One that will, can be for the people.
Turn the coin carefully look at the other
side. We have elected all your presidencies
given you our power all the while. Are you
ready America.

Are you ready my black brothers?
Are you ready my black sisters?
You are a motivator, challenger creating
changes. Fears, fears, fears, fears. Creating
anxiety, anxiety, anxiety. Stimulating
stimulating logically stimulating society. You
are labeled a bastard. A woman forced to have
a child abortion was not legalized. Abandoned by its
father. He is searching, exploring its roots. It's here
it's here. Your inheritance it's here. This land does
not belong to one creed. It belongs to everyone.
Free the black man, free the black man
Are you ready America.

Are you ready America? Are you ready white
America? We are willing to be your neighbor. But
are you willing to be ours? Wake up America, wake
up America. You have been sleeping too long. Wake
up America, wake up America unlink the slavery
chains that bound the black man. You have been

hurting, hurting, hurting him too long. You have been sleeping, sleeping, sleeping too long. You have been singing, singing, singing the same old song.

Are you ready my black brothers? Are you ready my black sisters? Tell me white America, we are always   Willing to be your neighbor but are you willing to be ours. Where are they who struggled. Where are they who educated you that we are not equal men, that your constitution we need to amend. Tons, tons, tons, tons. Weapons, weapons, guns. Guns, guns, guns, guns. Martin Luther was shot down. Marcus Garvey exiled threatened by blackmail and your guns. Blood, blood, blood, blood. Malcolm and Kennedy shot down. Tell me White America is the black man still your illegitimate child. You are abandoning him all the while. Are you ready America? Are you ready for the black presidency?

Are you ready my black brothers?
Are you ready my black sisters? White America we are ready to be your neighbor. But - are you ready to be ours. America, America, you have been holding the black man too long, with a greater intellectual bond, one that was not initiated by your genius slavery creator. I see another Hitler. I see another Hitler stretching out his hands. The man who you called a mad man. Eliminating his so-called inferior. Created a holocaust for the Jews to maintain a fantasy supernatural race. Tell me white America when will you free, free, free the

black man. Another ten decades after you eliminate him from your land. Wake up America you have been sleeping too long. Are you ready America?

Are you ready America?
Are you ready my black brothers?
Are you ready my black sisters?
Are you ready my white brothers?
Are you ready my white sisters?
I feel we are more than neighbors.
We are citizens of this American land.
A divided country can never stand.
Your enemies are aware they are making plans.
Your problem is in your own hands.
If you are united you will not be afraid of a communistic society. You have arms enough citizens enough to direct everyone. When you are strong, when you are one your enemies cannot infiltrate your land. Are you ready America are you ready for the black man? Are you ready America?

Tell me America why are you so afraid of the black man. Are you afraid of retaliation? Your perplexed conscience tells you; you have been holding on too long. Still! With a chain, one that is stronger than slavery bond. Educated him, gave him only substandard positions in your society. Excluding him from your political arena. Wake up America, wake up America wake up! Wake up! You have been sleeping too long. Isn't it time you free the black man - Are you ready America?

Fear! fear! fear! fear! anxiety rocks the mind of society. Changes, changes, changes afraid to create. Statistically scientifically, your research has proven that blacks do not have inferior genes. That he can compete with his white counterpart. A reformation should have given him, yet financially, educationally you still decide to anchor him. Retrospecting back to colonial rules, the black man was exempt from school. You hold the black man; you leach the black man. Is he a dog, you are so humane to your animals?

Do we still have to crawl colonial masters?
Wait for crumbs from off your tables.
Freedom, freedom free the black man.
Are you ready America? Can you realize that we are one? Citizens, citizens of this land who should be proud. Strong. Willing, willing volunteering ready to protect our native land prevent infiltration of the enemy's hands.
Are you ready, are you ready are you ready for white and black to be one? A divided country can never stand. Your enemies are aware they are making plans. Are you ready, are you ready -----Are you ready America? -----

Wake up America! Wake up America! Wake up America. Wake up! wake up! wake up! Wake up! You have been sleeping. Sleeping, sleeping - - sleeping too long singing, singing, singing the same old song. Are you ready for the black man?

THE FORCES THAT YOU AND I CANNOT CONTROL

The forces, the forces that we can't control.
Those forces that propelled the writer to pick
up his pen after he tucked himself to sleep
The forces, the forces that you and I cannot control

The forces the forces that we cannot control.
The forces that lead the messenger to deliver
The message whether it be snowing lighting
Raining or thundering. The forces the forces that
you or I cannot control

The forces the forces that we cannot control.
The forces that mold you shape you construct you!
Give man a mind to think superbly over
All animals creatures on this vast land.
The forces the forces that you and I cannot control.

The forces the forces that we can't control.
The forces that resurrected Jesus Christ from the
tomb. Led Paul down the Damascus Road.
Delivered Jonah from the whales belly. Rejuvenated
the strength of Samson that was taken. The forces
the forces that you and I cannot control.

The forces the forces that we can't control.
The symbiotic forces that unite the love of a Mother
and child. The forces that whale her belly when he
suffers. The forces, the forces that you or I cannot
control.

The forces, the forces that brings people together,
from the first moment they lay eyes on each other.
And even sometimes when they hate each other the

forces still bring them together. The forces, the forces that you or I cannot control.

The forces the forces that we cannot control.
The forces that plague our dreams turn fantasy into reality. The forces that make a baby walk
The forces that make a baby talk, smile cry or even laugh. The forces, the forces that you or I cannot control.

The forces, the forces that we cannot control.
The forces that make your decision while asleep. The forces that make your enemy conquer you and in turn it exalts you. The forces, the forces that you or I cannot control.

The forces, the forces that we can't control.
The forces that will deliver you although snares are laid to encapture you. The forces that will let the Black Man regain his pride dignity and fame so that he will be proud to say the name AFRICA! Mother Africa the land from which we came. The forces, the forces that you or I cannot control.

The forces, the forces, forces, forces can you feel the forces can you see the forces can you touch the forces. Forces, forces, forces, rapture, forces rapture. Forces, rapture, rapture, rapture, rapture, forces. Forces, forces, forces, forces the forces that you or I cannot control.

THE UNCONCEALED TALENT

Treasures from my heart
Pleasures from my mind
Within this book memorable
Knowledgeable works of art confined
Hoping to be shared with
All mankind, to enhance beauty
Relieve suffering give a sense of
loving sharing care. Through the
strategies of assertiveness adjusting
compromission and love man will be
guarded from his own destruction.

CYBER CLERICAL ASSOCIATES, LLC
KISSIMMEE, FLORIDA 34744